Apprenticed to Justice

KIMBERLY BLAESER is a Professor at University of Wisconsin–
Milwaukee where she teaches Creative Writing, Native American
Literature, and American Nature Writing. Her publications include two
books of poetry *Trailing You*, winner of the first book award from the
Native Writers' Circle of the Americas, and *Absentee Indians and Other
Poems*, as well as a scholarly study, *Gerald Vizenor: Writing in the Oral
Tradition*. Of Anishinaabe ancestry and an enrolled member of the
Minnesota Chippewa Tribe who grew up on the White Earth
Reservation, Blaeser is also the editor of *Stories Migrating Home: A
Collection of Anishinaabe Prose* and *Traces in Blood, Bone, and Stone:
Contemporary Ojibwe Poetry*. Her most recent critical publication is a
100-page essay on Native poetry, "Cannons and Canonization," in
The Columbia Guide to American Indian Literatures of the United States.
Kim lives with her husband and two young children in the woods and
wetlands of rural Lyons township Wisconsin.

Apprenticed to Justice

poems by

KIMBERLY BLAESER

SALT

CAMBRIDGE

PUBLISHED BY SALT PUBLISHING
PO Box 937, Great Wilbraham. Cambridge PDO CB1 5JX United Kingdom

© Kimberly Blaeser, 2007

First published 2007

Printed and bound in the United Kingdom by Lightning Source

Typeset in Swift 9.5/13

ISBN-13 978 1 84471 281 6 paperback
ISBN-10 1 84471 281 8 paperback

Salt Publishing Ltd gratefully acknowledges
the financial assistance of Arts Council England

For Tony Blaeser, 1912–2005.
Whose songs have filled my years.
Who sings on.

For all to whom I live apprenticed.

Contents

Acknowledgements

Miigwech to the friends, family, and colleagues who have supported me in my work.

To my many relatives whose lives and stories have sustained me through the years and whose advice, humor, and companionship continue to feed my spirit, I send these words as gifts.

Thanks to those who offered comments on portions of this manuscript, who provided inspiration for specific poems, or who hosted me at conferences and readings. Particular thanks to Amy DeJarlais, Phong Nguyen, and Janet McAdams for editorial feedback, and to the people of Kirkenes, Norway for hospitality and the most awesome of performance venues at the Barents Spectacle. A happy sigh of gratitude to my writerly friends with whom I share this journey. Thanks especially to members in my cyber writing network.

Thanks to my friend and child caregiver, Beth Picazo; and to the many poet caregivers with which I am blessed—Len, Amber and Gavin, Tami, Robert and Lenor, Naomi Barnick, Mary and Doyle Turner, and the host of others who provide everything from long telephone laughfests to carpools while I am away. To students, old and new, from whom I continue to learn.

Thanks to the Wisconsin Arts Board and to the UW-Milwaukee College of Letters and Science for support to undertake research, travel, or writing.

I also offer my sincere thanks to the editors of the various journals, websites, and anthologies in which some version of a number of these poems previously appeared:

Sweeping Beauty: Contemporary Women Poets on Housework; Sister Nations: Native American Women on Community; Eating Fire, Tasting Blood; Imaginary (Re-) Locations: Tradition, Modernity, and the Market in Contemporary Native American Literature and Culture; Traces in Blood, Bone, and Stone; Other Voices International Project.

Modern Haiku; The Cream City Review; Valparaiso Poetry Review; Studies in American Indian Literature; Free Lunch; Rosebud; Third Coast Review; Cold Mountain Review; Pembroke Magazine; Yukhika-látuhse.

i.

The turn we take. One direction. Another. Never a single source. For any journey taken. Or taken on. As if it were a duty or a gift. Something passed to us. This strange map drawn of blood or history. As if we could possess it. Or them. Not like a quality of light. Or shadows. In which we travel. As if possessed.

Family Tree

A boxer grandfather
who once fought Star Bad Boy
who sired six beer drinking German sons
all with the same big hands.

The grandmother I never knew
who might be responsible
for the heft of my thighs
is for certain the origin
of my father's sauerkraut
and fine venison sausage
perhaps for his sweet tooth
and maybe mine, too.

My father who turned those boxer hands
to percussion and gesture
tapping and clapping and snapping
the quickstep songs
but buttercupping the fingertips
to croon on bended knee
the long drawn *Mona Lisa,
Mona Lisa, men have loved you.*

My Chippewa grandmother
who was a midwife and medicine gatherer
tiny twig of a woman
who bore twelve children
bore the loss of two babies to influenza
the loss of one grown son to white man's war
and the loss of a generation
limbo Indians turned to alcohol.

My Indian grandpa
who squints darkly
into cameras of the past
who raised two generations
on rocky bottom allotted land
twenty-eight slow horse miles
from the village store
his crinkled story eyes
my first memory at two.

My mother born of dawn
in a reckless moon of miscegenation
whose foot rode the pedals
on fifty years of Singer sewing machines
her needles dancing rituals on a ribbon shirt
blending our jagged mismatched edges in a crazy quilt.

Two uncles who ran away
from Pipestone
Indian boarding school
and an auntie who stayed
who lost her fingers
saw them caught mangled
in the laundry press
who beaded kneaded quilted and braided
her way through four children
just the same.

Houses and fish camps full of cousins
who rotated authority
on marbles sex and skunk etiquette
whose probation blues and 49 songs
deprived me of bee stings broken bones
swimmers itch drunken despair
and suicide
in whose tangled litters
blonde and black-haired softball players
I fearlessly set down my suckling babies.

My great grandfather *Nii-Waan*,
Mii-nii-waan-noo-gwosh, Lover of Natural Things,
whose Antell heart I am said to bear
who carried his name with humbleness
as I try to
and sometimes with rage
fire brown eyes sharp as any weapon
who cupped his hands around fertile seeds
brown fingers the pinecone
shelled house of protection.

All my relations.

Shadow Sisters

We could meet them bent over the bait bucket, or feet glued to the pedals of a sewing machine. We could watch them legs crossed desperately, hobbling off laughing in the direction of the woods or the outhouse. Or find them walking midnight floors with an infant who mews its feverish approach to truth.

Cooking food they couldn't afford, smoking away a new coat, never weighing the raw balance of annuity or affection. Dark hair, dark eyes, dark skin, bruised lives they neither earned nor much took notice of. Children guarded, their treasured coins of hope.

Sixty-four years they trade kindnesses, gossip, jealousies. We watch them play saint and sinner, switching roles at silent cues. They are sisters. As different as one snowflake is from the other; as much the same. Somewhere in that space between likeness and dissimilarity eternity burns. Somewhere a feuding protective devotion. Two sisters, unmindful of the mark of history. *Laugh carelessly daughters. Rock wildly upon the lap of story.*

1951.

Together they drove an abandoned boyfriend's pickup truck 270
miles on the back roads between St. Paul and Nay-tah-waush.
Because neither could steer, clutch and change gears
simultaneously, they traveled locked together in a bizarre
version of a three-legged race, one steering and braking, one
clutching and shifting. Dripping with the sweat of fear, they
cursed and cried their way into a new syncretism, were baptized
into a laughing grace that ever after revisited them in times
of crisis.

1953. 1955. 1959.

Birth years. *When you play you pay,* they joked, swaddling
the fussy longings of youth, wrapping them tightly with
the responsibilities of babies, Minnesota heating bills, and
beer battles.

1965.

Toes sink into cold tilled reservation soil. Seeds sift through
fingers. They are women planting dreams with dank names like
rutabaga and kohlrabi. Extending their own black turnip feet
under the icy hose all summer. Stocking the hollow fall root
cellar. Filling canning jars with the colors of summer, the scents
of winter suppers: purple pickled beets, golden corn, eel-shaped
slippery jims, green beans, dill pickles, sauerkraut. Arranging
them on shelves late at night; gifts upon an altar.

1967.

One construction worker, one daddy, one volatile lover crushed
by a North Dakota night train, buried deeper than memory.
Three-legged, the families limp on.

1970.

Giddy games of canasta played too late into autumn nights
when everything is on the verge of falling. Decks of kittens and
mountain scenery mixed madly together, wild cards and red
threes coveted like someone else's husband. Children and
parents learning math, adding game points and allegiances.

1973.

Wounded Knee Indians scowl into cameras on every channel.
Five-time election judges, these sisters know tribal politics never
change. Indian dreams for justice stillborn these many
generations. But there is a restlessness that settles now beneath
their chests, fluttering like the first movement of small life
within a woman's body.

1977.

Driving together again, thermos of coffee and cigarettes
between them, they make five a.m. departures for electronics
assembly line jobs seventy-five miles away. Return for late night
bartending. Everything just another road trip leading back
home. To picnics and birch bark Sundays, croquet and crappie
fishing. To children who come and go in their own frenzied
migrations, anchored by that same whispered weight of longing.

1980.

At the horseshoe bar, old flames surface behind the moist amber
of a beer glass. Everyone acts like they are still in love. In a hard
week, sleep comes more easily if they pretend they believe it.
Sometimes in the cold of January, they forget they are
pretending.

1982. 1985.

In the polyester years they become grandmothers. Sisters dizzy
with the time-lapse passage of their lives, they brush wisps of
hair from wrinkled foreheads, from still nut-dark eyes, as if they
could dispel the bewilderment of rebels falling into grace. At
last, courting the danger of acknowledgement, over fish entrails
or quilt pieces they puff out small questions, see them rise and
expand like smoke rings. Gray circles hover between them,
truant halos never asking *How much?* or *How many?* But *Why do
you suppose? How come?* And *What we gonna do?*

1988.

Losses multiply as first a knee joint goes, then the good ear. The
last parent, one brother, two nephews, three women friends
from way back when. When the roll of reservation dice take
their toll, old hearts still break.

1992.

Shooting Star. Northern Lights. Firefly Creek. They visit all the
casinos. Indians everywhere are coming out, celebrating 500
years of survival. These women have been out their whole lives,
know survival like a long hangover. Tastes like castor oil
sometimes or like bitten-down tears, but it's been getting easier
to swallow every year. Sweet like maple sap when you see a child
off to a new growth tribal college.

Legacy is not a word these sisters use. Their English doesn't bend
to it. Still they wear the strands of history like strings of colored
trade beads. Memorial days they visit all the old graves. Keep the
names from rusting on the tongue. Teach their children to
welcome the repetition of stories.

Like that they notice other reservation sisters. Mismatched and
inseparable. Watch when one half falls away. The other left out
of step, lost, unable to recognize her lone shadow. Two sisters
sharing the comfort of community gossip, they mourn each
separation, silently foldaway fear of their own. Each plans to live
longer, to spare the other the grief and loneliness.

Years bend around this pact. They wake in the new millennium,
not certain if they are still surviving or just the ghost spaces
that waver in time, markers shimmering with the significance
of past lives. Thought we saw them just the other day sitting
together outside the new clinic, one still smoking to keep the
piety of age at bay. *Joined at the hip.* That's what my sister says.

A Boxer Grandfather

Large-knuckled arthritic hands
that once knew power and speed
sparring, faking—a pair of rabid bats—flying
to meet the startled jaw of each opponent.
Once-dancing feet slide flat across floors
toes scouting each divot and curb;
Ninety-two-year-old bones afraid of falling.

A boxer grandfather who walked a beat
in the almost-frontier town where I grew up.
City cop when authority twirled a billy
when the law and lawless duked it out.
His arc of vengeance spinning
the rainy day stories of my youth:

> *Grandpa's ninetieth birthday. My mom was having a beer with him,*
> *when Pete Blaeser owned the pool hall. Some guy with too much gunpow-*
> *der in his pants and too much 3.2 in his belly was hanging around.*
> *Poking at my mom like a hungry woodpecker. Disregarded the old man*
> *on the bar stool. That was his mistake.*
>
> *One minute Ben Blaeser was a half-blind ninety-year-old with a cane*
> *across his knees. Then flashes that sweet fist, fired by its memory of youth.*
> *One drunk farmer hits the deck, went down with a soft thud. Grandpa,*
> *spinning his stool back into the present, brushes his fingers across my*
> *mom's forearm. A squeeze for reassurance, a wink. They go on with their*
> *two-handed solitaire.*
>
> *She lets him cheat all afternoon.*

An old boxer and a beat walker
he kept his legs his feet moving,
kept the square-dance songs
echoing in the empty barns of age,
pulled himself up and up after falls
wore cuts and bruises like badges.
Those still strong fingers gripping
shaking hands in long lines at funerals.
How you been, Ben?

A grandfather whose wrinkled boxer hands
opened to unveil Juicy Fruit, nickels and dimes,
who carried the invisible past to our door
packaged in crates with ruby red grapefruits.
A German grandfather, lean, silver-haired
still dreaming in the language of his youth.
A grandfather suspicious of bankers and soft beds.
lunches on limburger, soup and strong rye bread.
Year after year those boxer hands
rest heavy
cup my head like a cane handle
long fingers nesting deeper
and deeper still crooked blue veins spread
swim like narrow Danube fingerlings
beneath the golden strands of my hair.

Mashkawapide*

My Uncle Ike
nine months a twin
who came lonely
bearing two souls
in the hazelnut depths of his eyes
lived with twice the heart
double the heat of reservation boys,
driving buckboard and canoe
searching for clues
searching beer parlors and beaver lodges
for the doppelganger haunting his dreams.
Finally embracing his strange duality,
his demons withdrawn
like the $20 double eagle,
he stands
at the screen door of my memory
now holding
all worthless coins between his teeth,
his lips, pointing laughter,
speak into being my childhood names.

*Ojibwe: to be tied together

Jingles You Made
(for Bill Antell)

Cut from tobacco tins
snuff lids and coffee cans
bent round and pounded
silver cones *tinkle*
against red
jangle one against another
as I dance in the June sun
place my feet just so
finding the rhythm
of the drums
as each tiny metal cymbal
clinks in time
dangling from the ribbons
on my fawn brown dress
they swing and *jingle*
at my step
silver cylinders *singing*
and my moccasins tap in and down
move evenly
around the arena to the *song*
circling and again
now beneath my hair
sweat *trickles*
as passing the stand
I glance up
catch your eye
the *twinkle* there
so much
like a sound
we made
together
ho

The Womanless Wedding

He will tell you he was a mess sergeant
a square dance caller
a pile driver, pool hustler
and a poker player.
Some say he was a dandy
fancy white belts and drawers full of ties.
He may say he was a hula dancer
in a womanless wedding,
and I will believe him.

For though I have seen him sit
hand closed to strike his breast
at each peal of the Angelus bell,
lips mouthing his silent recitation,
I have seen that same hand
cupped lightly
around the puck at a shuffleboard table.
With body rocking and fingers caressing,
his hand slides that metal disc
gently floating the silver
ahead and back on the sawdust
pulling it close, then spinning it
swiftly powerfully   away
his aim sure
his arm following
and the song he hums
never stopping
until the beer glass touches his lips.

So if he says he played basketball
against the Harlem Globetrotters
and won,
I know it is just possible.
Possible that the man who recites from memory
The Rime of the Ancient Mariner
has long forgotten his children's ages
and his own confirmation name.

And even if I had not seen
those black and whites
of a young blonde man
holding a koala bear,
I would not doubt his stories
of New Guinea and Australia
nor his account of malaria
and coming home to another man's baby.

Too often I have watched
those tired blue eyes
stare through the pinprick holes of age
struggling to find coins, silverware,
door handles, the washroom;
trying hard to recognize faces,
to sort ones from twenties,
the lost dead from the living,
searching sometimes in desperation
to recall the wildest, the sweetest,
the most familiar legends from another century
of the boy who skipped three grades
in the white clapboard country school,
of the man who fed me Rocky Mountain oysters
and gave my dog beer.

Mornings that man sits
nothing but coffee for company.
But ninety years is time enough
and I won't begrudge him
a womanless wedding

and other contradictions.

The More I Learn of Men's Plumbing

1.

This visit, a malfunctioning waterheater. The electrician exclaims over the machine's age; my father agrees: *"Turned 93 May 8th. Had a keg of beer."* He excuses himself to see a man about a horse. The repairman nods and a bill appears. House calls make half his business. *"This is at least a conversation piece if not an actual antique."* Of course it is; everything in the house is holding on by its fingernails including my father. His own plumbing has become a frequent, if not always popular, conversation piece. His eyes gone, he becomes confused, sometimes forgets which way to pee. New bathroom etiquette: don't enter without pail and bucket, disinfectant, a sense of humor.

2.

Daddy's gone off food. His pants slip their skin. We belt them tight while I walk the three-block main street in search of elastic waistbands. Now his taste is all in his talk. Today it's soups. Backyard vegetable. Split pea around a damn good ham bone. And his favorite: chicken with wide egg noodles. His old man's cheeks wrinkle with contented lust. Like Pavlov's dogs we salivate, smell it simmering four hours on the gas stove, its fat collected in oily pools at the top. Even in memory I am caught trying to siphon those away. As if he had read my mind, his mild reprimand comes: *Fat gives it flavor.*

3.

Now cushions pillow his ninety-three-year-old bones. The wooden
dining chair a pile of quilted adages. After cribbage, he turns to
other remembered pleasures. Music. Dancing. Fishing. And
women. For these he has retained the taste and the memory. The
equipment a little rusty, but the old charm still intact. Young or
middle-aged, they all take his hand, bend to hear his rhymes and
innuendos. Just now it's a short pixie cut with my mom's name.
Telling me of her light, he sighs. *Ah, if only I were forty years younger.*

MIA, Foreign and Domestic

He was perpetually missing
when I grew up.
My Uncle Clifford,
lost somewhere
between the life boat
and his downed ship.
"He made it out,"
reported his boyhood friend
turned military comrade.
"But he turned back
went searching, I guess,
for our missing men."

I still see him swimming
long stroke after long stroke
arrowing toward the horizon
of some far off ocean.
Propelled away
by that Antell trait—
is it pride or compassion?
that keeps getting us
into trouble
generation after generation.

And the veteran who returns
recites the melancholy story
at Kohler's tavern
on Friday nights,
a pack of Pall Malls rolled up
in the white t-shirt sleeve
of the arm that raises his glass:
"And I never saw him again,"
he lies
as the memory of Clifford Antell
parks himself on the stool
at the far end of the bar.

He was that stranger's head
half turned away in a crowd
somehow familiar.
The man I would walk toward
heart-thumping
already reaching out to tap
the shoulder of his navy seaman's jacket.
The one whose turning
full face
always meant disillusionment.

Even though the white cross
was placed over an empty grave
before I was born
and stone was carved
1925–1943
to enclose him,
I still regularly brought him home
as a valiant POW,
as fresh-faced hero
newly recovered from amnesia.

But I have since learned
that no injury or war
could cause any of us to forget
the names and stories that made us,
and that my Uncle Clifford
is still out there somewhere
swimming between a sinking ship
and a lifeboat
with destiny tucked
like a limp body
beneath one arm.

ii.

That which refuses pretension. Or travels on the wing of some other wisdom. For this we burn our offerings. In some lodge across that remembered bay. I can only follow the faint echo of a flute. But nevermind. I have lifted my pack.

Cranes flushed from a field
take flight; rusty hinge voices
call loudly, now recede.

Some Kind of Likeness

Again today it happened. At my feet I saw the grey bird wing, just one severed from the bird. Slight and curved in the remembered form. With my backward glance the texture unmasks itself, becomes a small fallen segment from a tree. The weathered wood surfaces from feathers. I stand before them—wing, wood, wing, wood, wing—back and forth. The grey shape drawn, erased, redrawn, hovering like bird or bark on the edge of realities. Holding the air-thin space between sight and vision.

The Spirit of Matter

Small nesting box on spindly pole,
solitary and still. This dark shape
cast once against the evening sky
once upon the green depthless water.
Too perfect an image
for the fragile reality of July in America.

I whisper past
but cannot leave the dark remembered shape.
Now I chance to see it unfold
changing from box to bird.
One squared corner unlocks—
my breath is rising like a phoenix.
As scissors beak leads head up
the small tube of its neck pulled, expands
into the infinity of this belief
and legs part
become separate
like once the waters of earth
pulled away
and cast us here to gaze.
Shore birds standing still as matter.

grace of crossings

silhouette of trees
evening sky
and somewhere between
a lace edge of infinity

together you stand watching
the world blow out its candle
chill of earth rising into your bare feet
heat of your bodies a third form between

a single hollow note
whistles gently in the purple night
while hands clasp
over the once fathomless dimension

now the tributaries—
swollen pipes of leaf
veins endless as life lines
pressed one against another

dusk mist transforms
into dawn dew
lays liquid between
the eyes of leaf and air

and even as sunlight
licks dry the night
the border still shimmers,
and this truant halo lingers

where onejoinsanother
where visionsoverlap
where lives come together

Somewhere on the Verge

Trees bobbing under the weight
of what cannot be seen.
The wind that carries the lilac
scent splays the leaves and
now we catch a glimpse
of golden feathers.

My hopeless and relentless pursuit
of the perfect photograph
the image always there late
or a second too soon,
the focus slipping away, now
gone the way of river water.

Or summer's wild strawberries:
star-white blossoms become tiny fruits—
hard, green, white, then *poof.* Stripped
by the birds who leave us just a taste
a pail bottom full of ripe red longing
each season, years on end.

Like the children's loud voices
crowing "I'm ready!" until dusk,
when you come in from cutting
too tall grass, fists full of flowering
garlic mustard—seed heads ready
to populate our whole gaseous planet.

And the striped-headed bittern freezes
bill pointed skyward, masking his presence.
Timid, teasing—it doesn't matter. Each yearning
held, keeps me, spilling words in pursuit,
like late night snoring from the back
of your throat takes me all the way to dawn.

Two Oak Stories

Walking Steele Road. Before me a red-tailed hawk glides silently through the leaf-scented air. Down from a tree on my right, it swoops. A curving flight lighted by autumn sun. The glorious fan open. He lands high in the oak on my left. Now watches me walk by. Corkscrews head; keeps me in sight. And I turn mine, pounding heart holding, hawk in my vision. Two watchers; some wordless exchange.

ii.

Catching slight movement. I look carefully at the burr oak, decide I have imagined something. Now my imagination gives a scolding chirp and the knot in the tree transforms into the face of a chipmunk. Poking his head out of a small hole, he continues his striped tirade. I watch as his tiny nose transforms, becoming the center of the knot, part of the twitching alive chipmunk face, the tree, the face, the knot, the life.

Gelatin tadpoles
sprout legs one two three, now four. Tail
going, going—frog!

Boundaries

Frontispiece:
Her white chest lifted from the water
wings spread and poised
on the loon edge of song dance or flight.

Ballet in endless acts:
Paddling a small bay on the Kawishiwi
River, we watch the four figures—
checker-backed and web-footed—
glide in classical lines through the waters
their slick feathers gleaming
as they swim or drop like sinkers in a dive
turning beaks and bodies with an instinct
of actors in a centuries-old drama.

Costume sketches:
Stark black and white checks repeat
diminish in intricate optical illusion
over the curve of the back
reappear wavering in the water's reflection.
Black bill and hyperbolic forehead
sweep towards delicately striped neck.
Intense beads of red dot the black head,
form doll-like eyes.

Dusky chicks hover
only a pencil sketch or poorly imprinted copy.
Faded shades of grays
check the back
under the disappearing down of the young.

Stage directions:
Twenty-inch wingspan of landing bird
planes against a backdrop of August green waters.
Chicks hug the sides of hen and drake,
swan their necks around their parents'
or paint themselves a shadow in their mother's wake.
Adults shield their young with their own bodies,
then plunge search and surface to answer
plaintive clucking cries of hunger or greed
for the small fish from their beak
the green vegetation pulled from the river's bed.

Postscript:
Yodeling old world divers,
they trace with their sleek wet frames
a pattern borrowed from some lost memory of
an ancient watery existence
a rapture
where dark limbs slipped through cool passages
and the sun glittered on tiny waves of time
painted intricate honeycombs
or threw shadows on the dusk flat pond
of destiny.

Invocation:
Oh,
swim me to the Kawishiwi River bottom
and back.
Bear me on your fluted beak.
Teach me now to hold myself on the brink
now to cry in wild echoing abandon
Ahh-raw-rooooooooooooo.

Memories of Rock

At two, copper curls tumbling out of his Mickey hat, my son loved
to skip rocks or throw them *kerplunk* into the water. Sitting on
boulders at the edge of Farm Lake in the still cold spring BWCA
waters, we repeated rock stories. With the sun's rays humming
background, we searched for the skipping shapes, gathered piles
of grays, reds, and blacks, then shared or bartered our treasures.
He assigned great significance to throwing order and sequence, so
I would wait patiently and in fascination as he labored to explain
his ideas for our next launching. *Otay, Mama. Dis time it will be my
tune first when we count to free. Den you have to throw you wock and
skip it. Way out.* He began to worry that we would run out of rocks
on our little patch of beach. I explained in that fairy tale voice of
certainty that the lake would always bring us more, as stones
endlessly washed ashore and away and ashore.

As he became more discriminating, we began to wade into the
water to find our skipping stones, our baby drops, our big splash-
ers. After hours of this activity each day, I became quite bored
with it and only as attentive as his safety required. My thoughts
and vision strayed, following the angle of shipoke flight, lost in
the honeycomb patterns of ripple and reflection.

Then one afternoon I plunged my hands into the cold water
after a flat skipper and came up with a perfect triangle stone.
Small in my palm and smooth, tiny black mystery of story. As I
exclaimed at its pretty shape, Gavin immediately assigned it a
launch number in the next sequence. Although I resisted, he
insisted in a way that threatened to become an argument or an
episode of crying. Why I let that dissuade me from pocketing my
treasure, I still wonder. But I felt the absence in my fingers before
I understood the loss. Almost before the ripples had rung them-
selves out, I began hoping I might find it again. But, of course,
like all rocks—thrown or kept—it was gone. Swept away.

And now when we tell rock stories, I know that somewhere
beneath the floating illusion of surface, at the green-black
bottom of Farm Lake, sinking ever deeper into the soft silt, there
is a tiny black rock triangle, fleeting as happiness.

Listing Ecstatic

Morning after the rain and every glistening thing seems poised to delight.

One wind puff launches a bevy of helicopter seed pods. Showered with spring's exclamation points, I remember each one is worth a wish and so feel blessed, wishing as fast as I can.

Now air holds bird song. Feathered voices so syncopated or symphonic, filled with rapid trills and climbing an impossible range. And I with only one voice box and one tongue.

From this small hill, I trace May's spendthrift panorama. Fringes of prairie from which a blossoming tree rises up. Below, a white-fenced pasture and two apple-hungry horses that whinny a greeting. Down the serpentine country road where I will walk, and beyond to the dark tilled earth in the freshly rowed field of our farmer neighbor. Yellow specks of dandelion dance at the unplowed edge, and farther still a glimpse of wetland. Now honking from a V of geese. Seven against the sky, flying in, then arrowing toward the lush land that will be their table this day, as it is mine.

Drowned worms and tan-brown slugs, galactic antennae standing out distinctly on the wet pavement. The yet small green leaves knocked down by rain and wind. Wet, delicate, some lacy and multi-fronded, others the round spades of playing cards. I lift them, see their perfect form repeated, dry and a shade lighter against the damp black road.

Before me on the ditch grass, only steps away, four goldfinches. Yellow and black flowers of the air planted here for this instant. As they lift off, join a small flock in the pines, their bright shapes light the lime green of soft new tree candles. And impossibly, below the pines, explosions of purple violets.

Each tiny plot of ground, bursting, could fill my notebook, my day; the same ground where I see the morning dung from the neighbor's dog. Before a small plant I bend to where it hoards raindrops on the veined palms of it leaves. Olive green, streaked through with mauve, they glitter when the sun winks off the moisture. I feel long in the tongue, tempted.

Writing, I, too, curve myself into a vessel, wear turning shades of wonder, strive to glisten—this small way.

Drawing Breath

There is no purgatory like poetry
that won't be written
into stanzas lines words
that won't fashion some
catch between knowledge
and desire
between the cold cash of meaning
and the questions feathered
across my back
the small static contact
lifting the hair on my arms.

No one reads to me anymore.
At fifteen he still holds his finger
in the book
on the very page where we left off.
Nothing beckons like story withheld.

Something beyond that point
where dusk blue wavers
between mist and rain,
that faint animal calling
persistent yet indistinct,
something that slips
almost off the shoulder.

Not anticipation
or remembrance
but the very point
of any turning
as if
it weren't
a fine line
but infinite

in its thinness.
Not meaning
but almost,
not saying,
but the breath before.

Seasonal: Blue Winter, Kirkenes Fire*

December snow falls fumbling
through great drafts of memory
piling once more upon the backs
of the hunched and soundless old women.

Such age we cannot hold
in the wrinkled leather purses
of our eyes
in the black hollow of empty mouths.

Yet faintly we hear
time soughing in the darkening winter sky
pine ancient, winter song of sleep
echoing still in a callused crust—
this ceremonial remembrance:

Terra cognita, terra incognita.

There is a place in the distance
where the wintering land
and the cloud heavy sky
meet at the horizon of all knowing.

There is a lonely moment
when they become indistinguishable
dusk and day blending one into another
until the division between land and sky falls away

    and we stand

surrounded by the blue white world
bereft of every common marker
suspended somewhere between vision and reality
lost, snow blind
tumbling into a dimension
beyond where feet may stand
on these frozen border lands.

Terra cognita, terra incognita.

Then it is we wake chanting
through endless painted patterns of the dusk
in the time and timelessness
of what once were days
cut loose now from all equilibrium.

So soul rest comes upon the Nordic land
and upon its ancient reindeer people.
The tired water sleeps as ice
and we glide upon its hardened body
and slowly turn the earth with our prayers.

Then riding the accumulated vibrations of voice,
following the steam sign of our winter breath,
the warm globe of light returns.

Terra cognita, terra incognita.

We are born to know this moment of elation:
sun the fire that rises
over the ice white tundra of arctic winter.
Each year our lives revolve
as first earth turns its face
from the burning orb of sun,

and we in simple desperation
light the crackling signal fire
hold to its flames our icicle bodies
our feet the drum, stamping
the rhythm of renewal
calling sweet holy transformation.

Terra cognita, terra incognita.

What we know in darkness
we may forget in daylight,
and so cold may come upon our hungry souls
like a ritual,
medicine passage to rebirth.

This year and next and each to follow
transport us with every recited memory
instruct us in reverence
for the bright warm gifts of sun and fire.

Each year we stand on the brink
to ignite with the torch of our tongue's song
that which is withheld
that which strokes our longing
our hardened forgetful souls

Terra cognita, terra incognita.

Now the dark veil is lifted
we shed each inky fear
and walk as one to hail the source:
Oh sun, oh fire
Tundra flower of the winter night!
Open the red flames of your petals,
Waken this eternal drama of emergence—
death to life, dark to light, ice to fire.
Now enlighten us with all that is known.
Now enlighten us with all that is unknown.

Terra cognita, terra incognita.

We turn and face this burning truth—
Infinity in the darkened eyes of night,
Infinity in the flaming belly of fire.

*Kirkenes is a small city in the arctic region of Norway.

Rain-soaked snowman's scarf
sags, buttons fall one by one,
now off with his head!

Wild turkeys at field gate
dark hulks against late March snow
no strut just peck peck.

House Work

The hollow base of an old water pump. Inside, a nest takes shape.
Mother chickadee searches, then fetches and carries small twigs.
She lands nonchalantly on the handle, *poof* disappears down the
pipe. In the round belly before the spigot, four tiny lumps, new
lives that huddle and peep. Perfect black and gray chickadee
markings. Neck rings already visible. Even careful footsteps
arouse the sleeping birds. *Twittering* calls back the scolding
mother. Now protecting, now feeding her thumb-sized offspring.
She flies. Back and forth and back . . .

20 September

Grasshoppers
explode at my step.
Under weight of their abundance
fall dry corn crackles.
Then too wind rustles
through browning stalks
and cicadas drone steadily
across the whole golden landscape.

So much talk today:
my feet crunch the fallen acorns,
apples thud as they drop
and squirrels scold
the flags of their tails bristling.
Voles scuttle across the forest floor
and even the tiniest triangles of bird's feet
sound autumn leaves.

Ooh . . . Ahh!

The moon is a lopsided air balloon
bobbing just above the horizon.
My eyes pop. My heart goes flip-flop.
To watch this inflated orange neon
gobbled by night clouds.

Haiku Journey

i. Spring

the tips of each pine
the spikes of telephone poles
hold gathering crows

may's errant mustard
spreads wild across paved road
look both ways

roadside treble cleft
feeding gopher, paws to mouth
cheeks puffed with music

yesterday's spring wind
ruffling the grey tips of fur
rabbit dandelion

ii. Summer

turkey vulture feeds
mechanical as a red oil rig
head rocks down up down

stiff-legged dog rises
goes grumbling after squirrel
old ears still flap

snowy egret—curves,
lines, sculpted against pond blue;
white clouds against sky

banded headed bird
this ballerina killdeer
dance on point my heart

iii. Fall

leaf wind cold through coat
wails over hills, through barren trees
empty garbage cans dance

damp september night
lone farmer, lighted tractor
drive memory's worn path

sky black with migration
flocks settle on barren trees
leaf birds, travel songs

october moon cast
over corn, lighted fields
crinkled sheaves of white

iv. Winter

ground painted in frost
thirsty morning sun drinks white
leaves rust golds return

winter bare branches
hold tattered cups of summer
empty nests trail twigs

lace edges of ice
manna against darkened sky
words turn with weather

now one to seven
deer or haiku syllables
weave through winter trees

Northern follows jig
body flashes with strike, dive:
broken line floats up.

iii.

To travel with you. One story. Or another. The tap of your walking stick. Now fire stick. That fish we dreamed. Or lost. The same one that fills our bellies as you stir fire. With your stories.

Of Wind and Trees

The wind blows twitter and nonsense
I hear it whistle through my sleep
No wild night fantasy could rival
The lurid stories bending the heads
Of trees.

Fingers paused on keyboard
leaves fall outside my window
tumble onto page.

Told at Beartooth in July

Orange lichen on rock.
Silk-petaled carpet of wild flowers.
And blueblack slits
cut diagonally across snow.
This tourist scape
transformed
by shift of light,
repaints drifts in relief,
unveils cirques.
Crusted lips
of hardened snow,
ledges
beckoning
like fingers
to daring travelers.

Who would take that step
just beyond sense
that sometimes bears weight
sometimes not?
We all take it in our mind.
Surprised even there
to crash through
tumble
wildly in space
or destiny
landing perhaps
in another geography
or falling
swallowed by another dark
redrawn body.

This one feathered
black, sleek
as crow or story
and gliding easily
across valleys populated
with buttercups
and shooting stars.
Now landing.
Again on some edge
of being
weighted
with longing.

Sun through window slats;
stripes—light, dark—fall down my leg
conjure zebra skin.

Something Deep Like Copper

Behind the sun-warmed rock
lizard-like, I have become the ground.
You walk, grazing, rack down.
August tundra, backdrop for your dappled coat.
Then something long-buried
deep like copper
sounds in weighted hoof steps
gone hollow in my ears.

If I Laid Them End to End

That old guy with the muskrat soup
slurps it loudly from the ladle
Hoowah, pretty good stuff!
You shift your weight on the stool
raise the bad leg just enough
and retrieve the red bandana hankie.
Talk still spills like sunshine
over the knife-marred counter
as slowly you wipe the can
push the cloth back in your pocket
and cough down the grape pop
glancing at the bobbing black head
where it surfaced in the pot.

The burned farm. That hungry year.
The long walk from Strawberry Mountain
warmed now with the weight
of fresh butchered *wiiyaas* in your pack.
Mum's baking soda biscuits mixed and cut
lined waiting in the tin pan
like our little kids' faces at the window.
Sure took the wrinkle out of our bellies that night.

One opening day when those two old fishermen
ended up dunked clinging to the canoe.
The hunt for diamond willow,
beaver camp on Easter weekend,
the whitefish feeding on wax worms,
the string of crappies slipped from your hand,
the missing outhouse floor,
training *waaboose*,
feeding the least weasel,
tales from working on the ships,
from boiling sap, planting trees, pounding, carving,
and then the cigar box memories
of *those old time Indians*
who could really tell stories . . .

Indian in Search of an Entourage

He was an Indian
blown into town on a white girls' dream
wearing destiny like a ten-gallon hat.
Black hair spidered down his back
thin long lines of hair waiting to be touched
in the dark hours before her waking.

He was an Indian
Singer
Poet
Preacher
or Powwow Dancer.
He was an Indian Politician
Native Language Speaker
and All-Night Freedom Keeper.

Born brown enough or red
marble-hard eyes
steelies, purees, cat's eyes.
Thick-calved Indian runner
chasing the ghost of Jim Thorpe,
running down the rumors of rewards
that came for brown-skinned brothers
who could sing Indian
dress cowboy
talk justice.

Mascot without a ball team,
an Indian
in search of an entourage.
A not-quite new-age, not-quite for-sale
Indian
who could wear small fame so well
on his chiseled cheekbones.

Bizaan*

The door to that story
closed.
Nails bent in place
to secure it. . .

Like dark silver spikes
turned, slid away
late one night
hurriedly
to be first in the outhouse.

Door creaking
at the hinges
so much like sudden
night sounds
rapid wings
muffled shrieks
from the close
pressing poplars.

Stepping in then
sinking
deep
fast
down
into
terror.
And calling
in loud wails and sobs
for help.

Get me out!
I'm in shit up to my knees!

Ojibwe: be quiet

[62]

The story turns here
to laughter
and, of course
to rescue.
As heavy male
voices
then booted steps
approach
join the women
who stand tearing
sides aching.

And the putrid
wet scents
and brown horror
blow away
at the realization
that
you have fallen
yes
feet deep
but are pulled
one strong hand on each elbow
up, up
from a dark
sucking hole
vilely filled
with the stuff
of your own
dark and terrible
imagination.

Or maybe

the damp pale clay
and sand
that clings
to your clothes
has just now
traded realities.

Because
you do find
it
the dark smear
of excrement
just there
under the small nail
of the still shaky
right hand.

Or
think
you saw it
before you plunged
that crooked knuckle, too
down
into
the cleansing
basin
of murky
story water.

Page Proofs

A house of unmade beds
and my clock ticking *hurry.*
This conversation with L
in red ink
in the margins
of *hurry.*
Another scribbled note
over words and whose
will suffice to bring order
to these scattered silences
and half-eaten thoughts.
Mail keys pens books
bury pages—
the markings
where voices reside
beneath the blackened
alphabet hearts
of civil exchange.

Goodbye to All That

He could have taken you prisoner, of course
when our two tribes were at war
over whitefish and beaver territory
and the Anishinaabeg chased your Indian ancestors
from the woodlands he now brings you home to.
Or your Dakota relatives might have waged a war party
on their swift plains' ponies to avenge your taking
and bring you back from those uncivilized
they named in disgust the rabbit-chokers.
But those histories of dog-eaters and Chippewa crows
are just a backdrop now for other stories
told together by descendants of smallpox survivors
and French fur traders,
clan members of Wolf and of Water Spirit.
And now you gather,
trackers and scouts in new bloodless legal battles,
still watch for mark and sign—
for the flight of waterbirds.

ii.

Old histories that name us enemies
don't own us; nor do our politics
grown so pow-wow liberal you seldom
point out the follies of White Earth tribal leaders.
(Except of course for the time our elected chair
mistakenly and under the influence of civilization
drove his pickup down the railroad tracks
and made the tri-state ten o'clock news.)
And Sundays behind the *Tribune*
he seldom even mentions the rabid casino bucks
or gets out his calculator and with lodge-pole eyebrows
methodically measures beaded distances,
results of territorial lines drawn in your homeland.
And even though I have seen him sniff, glance over
he really almost never checks the meat in your pot,
nor reconnoiters the place of your rendezvous
just to be sure.

Railroad Song

A train is coming. Listen.
Its *streeeaam* of saxophone sound carries
along the night corridors
of one-stop-light midwestern towns.
The rhythmic sand-block shuffle
of its wheels *chug-chug-chugging*
ladder tracks up the rolling hill horizons.
A cymbal *screech* of brakes
leaves it panting in place
while *Portage . . . Winona . . . Red Wing*
is trumpeted at the deserted night stations.
Aaaall aboard lifts sleepy passengers
into narrow double berths
as the cars *jerk stop jerk stop* back into motion.
Rhythmic rocking drum thumps accelerate again
the black musical snake winding away
into northern forests and lakes.
Now its falling-flute-note *whiiistle*
reports its exit, recedes;
echoes hang on dark mist
fade *ooout.*

Stories of Fire

(for Karen Auvinen)

I.

We burn prairie in spring
hoping fire will ravage
those rampant colonizing plants:
reed canary grass, garlic mustard.
purple loosestrife.
Will call dormant seed
from earth's trampled memory.
Return coneflowers, prairie smoke,
little blue stem.
And that return shall follow
on the heels of return:
old prairie from fire,
butterflies, insects, ground-nesting birds
at the invitation of flowers and grasses;
even the small mammals
who prey upon the birds,
and us the large mammals
who feast on each bright color
purple violets, golden crest
on the puffed breast of meadowlark,
who drink in every strut of turkey
each shimmering warbler song.

Can this burning off
to some buried origin
ignite desire to rise
again
one layer
of life
at a time?

II.
My Isleta friend made medicine
that whole long day
as pain flared
in my scalded hand.
Ice, second skin, song,
barefoot beach walks,
the flick of dark hair and eyes—
pharmaceuticals
to prevent the worst
forms of scarring.

III.
You told me years later,
dropped it lightly
into another fish story.
Of your falling backwards
a long impossibly slow
drop over the back
of a clumsy dog,
into the gray coals
of that literary bonfire.
I heard it told again,
saw it written
in another's voice.
A tale of your outlandish
hospital humor,
laughing there on the edge
as the seed pod called spine
surfaced above blistered skin,
and burst
wildly and wonderfully o p e n.

And I think now and again
about Naanabozho
who brought us
this gift of fire.
That mythical trickster
whose own transformations
seem endless
even in our cramped imaginations
as he turns
from beloved
to betrayer
and back
and back
as each layer
of story is burned away
in the telling
as each dying meaning
reseeds itself.

This Dance

Listen.

She told it like a story
some silent spectator
standing for a giveaway
holding her prize high
in this strange arena of forgetting.
Hearing the song
my knees bend in reflex
like breathing, rhythm
the flypaper trap of remembrance.

Now in step now out.

Listening harder each year
to tribal drums muted by dissent.
Searching children's faces
for pattern, direction.
Like intricate stitches through seed beads
that space between missing teeth
is the breath we take
when we step in
step high and sure
tobacco closed in our hand.

Asemaa.

This moist offering
sticks to my heated skin
like old dreams and voices.
Step, step in.
Behind the moccasin pat jingle tap women
Behind the turtle rattle ankle bell men
Step step again step

In the circle you follow
Follow, lead and follow.
These sharp bruised edges of self

curve curve in

purple despair rounds
like floured fists punching down
raised puffs of bread dough.
Knuckles caress the cool white
until tiny gasps like breath
exhale in the yeast softness.

Now following

sound feasts, drum pats into song into
ribbon swirl shawl soaring wholeness
this slight step
joins joins in
a single footfall lifted and placed
touches and trampled ground slips away
this moment
in the dream of prairie grasses
in the sure steady rhythm
of every sovereign nation's dance.

iv.

No telling. What will anyone believe? In the aftermath of every war. I hear them talking. Just as the spring trees have swelled with words from each forgotten language. Someone still sings the songs. I listen.

Red Lake

When bullets sink into the flesh
of children,
color still matters.

After
Columbine,
left tattered
white middle class dreams
of immunity,
parents across this country
grieved enmasse,
blood pumped faster
in the crisp white shirts
of politicians,
and flag-waving citizens of every ilk
mourned and rallied
for change.

Columbine.
Melancholy ballad
Oh Columbinus,
in old school Latin
you are the flower dove.
Columba
turned hawk
gun-beaks and black flak jackets.
Your name
beneath full page photo spreads;
a chant
metaphor
purple call for change:
Columbine.

But even death
has a pecking order.
And the president
of a nation built
on soil soaked
with the blood of conquest
hesitates when he speaks
of sympathy
for the hapless young
who died in this
a reservation tragedy.

Add these children
to the anonymous
red dead of the Native Nations
of this America.
A twenty-first century America
who cannot waste its breath
to chant
the funeral song
for these fallen.
An America
who speaks this name
Red Lake
like an ethnic slur.

Red Lake.
Nagamon,
Red Lake.
Red Lake.
Mikwendam,
Red Lake.

Housing Conditions of One Hundred Fifty Chippewa Families*

White Earth Reservation, 1938:
wigwam
peaked lodge
bark house
tipi
log house
tar-paper shack
frame house
u.s. rehabilitation house.
sister hilger
you counted each one—
seventy-one tar-paper shacks,
eight united states rehabilitation houses
two wigwams
bark houses at rice camps—
you graphed
photographed
measured dimensions
calculated cubic air space
enumerated every construction detail—
23 with broken windows;
99 without foundations, buildings
resting on the ground;
98 with stove pipes for chimneys.
house, dwelling, place, structure—
home. Endaayaang.

* All italicized words are taken from Sister M. Inez Hilger's *Chippewa Families: A Social Study of White Earth Reservation, 1938.*

June to November
the year my mother turned five,
Mary Inez you walked these lands
the fervor of your order tucked
under one billowing black-sleeved arm,
amassing details of crowded quarters,
common-law marriages, miscegenation,
illegitimate children, limited education,
economic dependence on the WPA and CCCs
for charts that have outlived
those Anishinaabeg of the
one hundred and fifty chosen families.

Now you perch in my history
at one of *71 homemade or 79 factory-made tables*
sitting tall and precise on one of the *84 benches,*
49 backless chairs, or 81 armchairs,
or standing, Mary Inez, in the homes
of one of the *16 tar-paper-shack families*
or 8 frame-house families
for which you record *none*
under the heading of *chairs.*

Methodically you recite
like prayers of deliverance
each prepared question:
Why are these so many
unmarried mothers on the reservation?
Why are there so many common-law
marriages on the reservation?
What do you think can be done
to stop
the drinking to intoxication among the Indians?
I hear you interrogate each family

daily gathering indulgences
or ink smudged statistics
on what you label in caps *SOCIAL PROBLEMS*.
Any unmarried mother in the home?
Any intoxication in the home?
So dutifully you prompt each betrayal—
Father? Mother? Son? Daughter?
and then remind yourself, in print,
in a parenthetical aside
of the unreliability of the interviewee—
(Check this information
with some outside person.)
As if anyone then or now could forget
with whom resides the authority
for your social accounting

Ah, sister, I pity you
the prickly mystery of those questions
whose answers could not be checked
nor changed
by *some reliable outside person.*
So confidently you asked
Would you like to leave this home?
But *seventy-three per cent of the occupants*
of tar-paper-shacks on White Earth Reservation
in northwestern Minnesota in 1938
said no.
No matter, you wrote, *how dilapidated*
and inadequate the homes were,
the tar-paper shack families
were quite unwilling to leave them.

So they were asked again
asked another way
because *it was thought*
knowing the alternative
might change their mind:
Would you like to move into a rehabilitation
house; one of those fine new houses
the Indian Bureau built for the Indians?
But the negative answers grew.
Fewer still would think of leaving their home.
Not *thirty-five-year-old Anna,*
fifty-year-old Mary,
not *a widowed mother, sixty-one years of age,*
living on the outskirts of one of the highway towns,
not *Old Man Mink, seventy-eight years of age,*
nor *his wife, ten years his junior,*
who *agreed they liked their one-room shack,*
not *Mike, twenty-nine* and *a regular League of Nations,*
nor his white wife *Jane, twenty-eight,*
nor *their ten-year-old son.*
Gaawiin. Gaawiin niwii-naganaasiin.
Like *Jim, forty years of age*
and *Ella, thirty-eight,*
they wanted to stay
in the old ramshackled, tar-paper-covered homes.

And did you hear the bulrush psalms
of Gaa-waabaabiganikaag
as you painstakingly recorded each
softly intoned explanation?
And does the land remember you
Sister Inez, of the tar-paper-shack dwellers?
As surely it remembers Mary
who felt *well acquainted with the woods,*

or Anna, who believed she was living
more like the old Indian ways?
Somewhere in that *rolling land of rich loam*
is the adorned body of *Old Man Mink*
and perhaps somewhere roams the spirit
of the Midē wiwin elder who vowed
I'll stay right here. I won't leave here.
I've lived here too long.
I wonder, Mary Inez,
did your BIA-commissioned sojourn
in the land of white clay
somewhere lay its soul mark
looming crow dark
at the ruled edges of report ledgers
spilling into cautious recollection
even as the measured drip of black ink
might draw tabulations
upon white pages?

Before Minnesota winter winds
rattled the *162 full-sized, 104 half-sized,*
and 47 less than half-sized unbroken windows,
before that biboon nodin blew through
those *23 houses with cardboard-covered*
broken windows or blew through
your tight-lipped post-allotment spirituality
you returned to the Order of St. Benedict
and to the list of standards set out in 1935
by the National Association of Housing Officials,
those standards against which all our measurements
fall short, become sub—sub-standard, sub-human.
You left Mary Inez, the Latin Mass
and rosary zipped safely in one pocket—
the names of each Midē wiwin elder
drumming and chanting in the other.

Dictionary for a New Century

What would *housework* mean
to women who haul water from springs,
use lye soap and scrub boards,
who hang flypaper on ceilings
and sew cloth cupboard curtains
on the family treadle machine?

What does *kitchen appliance* mean
to those toasting bread in ovens
of old wood stoves,
or *bathroom appliance*
to those donning snow boots
to walk to the outhouse?

Somewhere between microwave pancakes
and the *state-of-the-art* mixmaster
I trip over the kitchen slop pail
retch at the smell of lard rendering.
Just as my fingers settle on the dvd remote
I remember to empty the ash can.

At three my daughter kisses and releases her fish
at four she asks if chicken is a dead bird.
At forty like Billy Pilgrim I come unstuck in time
still wait to take my turn in a three-foot washtub,
then light candles and soak in a warm whirlpool
now camped uneasily between *progress* and *nostalgia*.

With a heavy duty vacuum and a lightweight canister
I cruise the air-conditioned floors of my house
sweep away unearned *guilt* or hire a cleaning lady.
With electric everything and my computer whirring
I *work* my way through memories and philosophies
Try to recollect that proverb about idle hands.

What does *convenience* mean in a country of prosperity?
Should we use or release our histories?
Can *education* repay old debts?
If *science* and *technology* are the answers
who have we hired to ask the questions?
And what was it you said about *women's work*?

The Things I Know
(for Milwaukee Indian Community School Students)

I.
Just pay attention
to the way your hands move
in rhythm with your legs,
the way rabbits
multiply to the seventh year
and caribou change their migrations
following the food cycle,
and remember
how every part of creation
has relationship and rhythm
and walk that way if you can.

II.
Say to yourself this one thing:
Go on tiptoe and don't talk.
Then hush your thundering words
let them leave you
receding like footfalls
on sodden grasses of pilgrim ways,
until you learn stillness
and feel the butterfly flutterings
of matter against spirit,
light on water and water on light,
color changing to color changing
to change.

III.
You need no permission
to run faster than the pages turn
farther than crooked lines of type
on treaty documents
beyond the erasures of culture.
You need no permission

to run past the language banks
of stereotypes: Hiawatha, Pocahontas, Geronimo,
to run past the stolen medals
of the Sac and Fox Jim Thorpe
still running into history bereft.
You need no permission
to join with the dawn runners
like some imagined Abel.
You need no permission
to run to run—
You need no permission
to *stop running.*

IV.
And what you give away
is the very thing that makes you stronger.
Train your energy in blue-collar labor
muscles harden bones regain stature
and enduring becomes endurance.
Spend your voice in song,
daily your vowels round through
wind tunnels, scaling ranges
of sounds, echoing into canyons
of rising hallowed tones.
So enter the circle of brokenness
give everything you value
giveaway give back and away
wait for nothing and everything
will return:
so it happens in circles.

Who Talks Politics*
(for Heredia Peltz)

This is a poem for Heredia Peltz
whose slight shoulders curve
dance beneath her fringed poncho
with the grace of generations.
Heredia Peltz who teaches at Bruce Guadalupe
community school in Milwaukee,
who was memorialized
in carefully constructed English
by the students in her seventh grade class:
a Wisconsin woman making history.

Esperanza Antosanti, Luis Martinez,
Clarissa Banda, Noel Saavedra,
Gabriella Torres, Ernesto Lira,
Maria Isabel Rodriquez,

And Heredia Peltz
tiny dark volcanic force of freedom
erupting with regularity
in classrooms and community halls.
Teaching by her story and her life
that even the poor have choices
that strong dark women can stamp out pathways
in the mud black alleys
of race hatred and cultural bias.

Ivan Mendez, Ana Galeno,
Andrew Arroyo, Alex Pacheco,
Rafael Acevedo, Vanessa Gutierrez,
William Antonia Matos Sanchez,

* Heredia Peltz was recognized by the University of Wisconsin-Milwaukee's
Women's Studies program honoring "Wisconsin Women Making History"
when her 7th grade students wrote essays about her life and work saying,
among other things, that she "talks politics while teaching English" and
that she gave up a law career in order to devote herself to teaching.

And Heredia Peltz
who studied the laws
which did not keep her people
from living with injustice.
Who left the halls of illegality
to spend her words
on the lives of the children.
Heredia Peltz
who bothers to spell liberation
for students who must learn
each word in two languages.

Jasmine Rena Varela, Joe Padron,
Alma Ramirez, Jose Ornelas,
April Isabel Aponte, Dennis Campos,
Ali Sandra Marie Santiago,

And Heredia Peltz
passing a legacy of liberation
to the next generation,
Heredia Peltz
this Wisconsin woman
making history,
Heredia Peltz
who talks politics
while teaching English
to her seventh grade class.

Fantasies of Women
(for Carol Marefka)

They say:
there was an old woman
who lived in a shoe—
children, spanking, bed, no food
it's an old story,
one to rival the Peter tale
who kept his wife in a pumpkin shell,
or Jack Sprat who coveted
all the 90% lean cuts of meat,
while his ever-expanding
squat round wife
tumbles over the sides
of a tiny kitchen chair
over-filling the page
on which she is drawn.
We keep turning that page
but one caricature follows another.

Some claim:
women always were the delicate sex—
fainting, timid, helpless souls
you know that line
the length and breadth of those
whose names have scrambled
the letters of femininity
into unrecognizable derivations
Annie Oakley, Gloria Steinem
Wilma Mankiller
Rigoberta Menchu
Mother Teresa of Calcutta.
In pants or full veil
in every state of dress or undress
Cher's navel
the jewel on Cleopatra's forehead
burn like all beacons of dissent.

I heard:
A nation is never defeated
until the hearts of its women
are trampled upon the earth—
this one I believe
for I grew up among women
who could swallow a raw heart
whole or in infinitesimal pieces
deer heart, rabbit heart, turtle heart
and did swallow and chew
chew and swallow their own red hearts
beating *for survival*
   for survival
   for survival
   for survival.

And this is the single story
we write with our lives
women of travois, ox, or minivan,
of African brown barefoot toes
bound Chinese feet
or seventy-five dollars a pop Birkenstocks.
Together we walk on our houses of history
track true
the paths of indentured servants,
girl babies slain and buried,
this black dirt of bias exposed
overcome in
story cycles of scarlet fecundity
told through the fires of many tongues
and translated again
in the labor of women.

Now we sing:
There was a young woman
who lived in a shoe-obsessed
commercialized overstocked world
she had many children
and knew just what to do—
raise them to share the burdens
of all the people
to unearth the fantastic lies
they were taught to walk upon
to devour fear
chew and swallow
and to cast their hearts
for survival.

V.

Gone. Or gone on. Again. I see you lift your bad leg into the boot.
Her hand rises slowly like memory to the good ear. His ankle
brace stands empty by the picnic blanket. Someone laid a spirit
plate. That was one gesture. These dark words another.

What They Did by Lamplight

Clean rice, hand stitch
make pies, roll jingles
patch jeans, shake dice
clean fish, roll cigarettes
read from *The Farmer.*
Braid rugs, mend nets, tell stories
write letters, bead, cut quilt squares
boil swamp tea, deliver their babies.
Darn socks, peel potatoes, drink coffee
shuffle cards, cut hair, can tomatoes
sift flour, bead, sing church songs.
Scrub socks, gossip.
sing country songs
make tobacco ties
braid sweet grass
prepare their dead.
Beat frosting
laugh
embroider
crack nuts
depill sweaters
wipe their tears.
Search penny jar for old coins
shell peas, cut birchbark patterns
thread matching buttons together.
Build fire, make soap, join their hands
knead bread, read seed catalogues, smoke
slice apples, squeeze color into margarine.
Change diapers, shuck corn, soak beans
rock their children, boil water, crochet doilies
clean sunflower seeds, can dill pickles.
Sharpen knives, eat, iron
dance together
nurse their babies
remember their dead.

Refractions
(for Bill Harrold)

Why should it happen
that the smallest
zig-zagging black cricket
one stick leg raised—
a musician's baton,
holds and then releases
the same song
as my canoe paddle
slicing into glass?

Boundary Water's evening lake
still, mirroring
like memory doubles
you here and gone
now leaning akimbo
a cricket musician
message encoded in meter
in the rhythm of my own arms
paddling side to side
as if I could find you
in the funnel of each stroke
in the blue sluice of time.

And light grabs my breath again:
peering into that one space
where ledge rock dissolves into color
cascades grey and rust and moss green
effortlessly transforming at water's edge
tumbling headlong into repetition
unfolding mirror image
into the depthless eternity of reflection
until, in that moment, I forget
which side of vision
is mere reality.

And that this bent black line of insect
can sing
and more—that every chirp should count
in precise degrees
just how cold is loss.

Crunch of booted feet
on still frozen ground carries
across pond, echoes back.

Resisting Shape or Language

Perhaps I saw you best
across breakfast tables or diner counters
some small distance from conference conversations
in whimsical recitations of country western lyrics,
perhaps in the words
squeezed
between the opening and closing
of elevator doors
on the way to identities we might assume
in the fractured
consolation of public admiration.

Death isn't a story for me
to be rehearsed with each telling
disappearance reappearance remembrance
not an AP report nor NPR news flash,
I stumble awkwardly with the public spoken
all my words turn inward
to be whispered in darkened rooms
poured out to the scarlet upholstery
of a rental car.

What I collect that resembles memory—
small wrinkles in newspaper profiles
ellipses in authority
the day Milwaukee piled shoulder high
and the reluctant crooked smile
a line never written
but worn
and one you bothered to repeat
when I could not hear
above the applause of a life
you spoke over.

Weavings For Cousins Who Died Too Young

Bodies braided—leg waist leg—
we held tight on tire swings,
listened across the years
at the same floor vent
to overheard family secrets.
On worn paths criss-crossing
our shallow idyll of childhood
I trace deliberate markers, follow you
to fall hazelnuts, abandoned cars,
the spring itch of poison ivy.

Tireless magpies, we scavenged—
slingshots, quilt pieces,
fishing line, marbles and all glittering treasures;
feathered our nest with youth's whimsical flights
on rattling bikes and leaky green rowboats.
Built of the discarded some imagined
province—*now I lay me down*
in the old hollow among the skittering
squirrels and last fall's leaves,
I prepare a place for you in the abandoned
frame of an unfinished tool shed—
where our shadows still sit
over rainwater and mud pies
even as we stand together
at weddings—arm shoulder arm—
eat over the same wood fire,
hand one another our babies
in some old-fashioned blood pact.

And this is why I weep
at your leaving us all too soon.
Your name still ready
on my lips,

our last conversation
never finished—
the race car story and the cane handle,
plans for the turtle bracelet,
something about a bear near your house
and the mass of some cold anger
disguised as blue ankle weights
that tire you as you walk
from the back bedroom to the kitchen table.

Too simple to say
I will remember you
although I could never forget
our madcapped race
across the thawing lake,
water splashing up
from the tires—danger laughter danger.
Your delicate carvings
in antler dangle at my ears,
the diamond willow staff hangs
at my library window.
And though I never retained
the secret to cracking
a brazil nut whole
I still fumble for that
magic position,
see your long thin fingers
hold it just so—thumb, nut, forefinger—
and the simple breaking open
that luscious meat of memory.

And this, my cousins,
is what I mean to say:
I hold so many common
objects within the shadow
of your lost bodies.
Search the thin edge of reality
where loam turns on the point of a spade.
Now images flash at the corner of my eyes:
steam rising from the sugarbush kettle
above the tipped black bill of your hat,
that slight tease in the lift of your chin,
the house of cards rising rising at your deft touch,
and the rhythmic turning of the willow switch
with the slow roasting of meat and story.

Now I hear the lonesome shrill of the catbird
hidden cry from these small woods
and shivers wake to his lost-child's call.
But I have known other birds—
cranes, partridge, eagles, crows—and my magpie cousins.
In that thin air-walled play
house of our imagined lives
I turn again to hoarded treasures
crooked nails, burned sparklers,
dented commodity cans holding sweet wild grasses and flowers.
And because I have know other fragile houses
pegged at the corners with only hope,
I weave these words
like the empty cupped nest
fashioned of our entwined hands—finger finger finger—
your rough callused palms
still pressed against mine—touch absence touch.

July 29, 2002
Tijeras, New Mexico

Small nest of voices
keen beneath Sandia range—
sometimes warriors fall.

Apprenticed to Justice

The weight of ashes
from burned-out camps.
Lodges smoulder in fire,
animal hides wither
their mythic images shrinking
pulling in on themselves,
all incinerated
fragments
of breath bone and basket
rest heavy
sink deep
like wintering frogs.
And no dustbowl wind
can lift
this history
of loss.

Now fertilized by generations—
ashes upon ashes,
this old earth erupts.
Medicine voices rise like mists
white buffalo memories
teeth marks on birch bark
forgotten forms
tremble into wholeness.

And the grey weathered stumps,
trees and treaties
cut down
trampled for wealth.
Flat Potlatch plateaus
of ghost forests
raked by bears
soften rot inward

until tiny arrows of green
sprout
rise erect
rootfed
from each crumbling center.

Some will never laugh
as easily.
Will hide knives
silver as fish in their boots,
hoard names
as if they could be stolen
as easily as land,
will paper their walls
with maps and broken promises,
scar their flesh
with this badge
heavy as ashes.

And this is a poem
for those
apprenticed
from birth.
In the womb
of your mother nation
heartbeats
sound like drums
drums like thunder
thunder like twelve thousand
walking
then ten thousand
then eight
walking away
from stolen homes

from burned out camps
from relatives fallen
as they walked
then crawled
then fell.

This is the woodpecker sound
of an old retreat.
It becomes an echo.
an accounting
to be reconciled.
This is the sound
of trees falling in the woods
when they are heard,
of red nations falling
when they are remembered.
This is the sound
we hear
when fist meets flesh
when bullets pop against chests
when memories rattle hollow in stomachs.

And we turn this sound
over and over again
until it becomes
fertile ground
from which we will build
new nations
upon the ashes of our ancestors.
Until it becomes
the rattle of a new revolution
these fingers
drumming on keys.

Lightning Source UK Ltd.
Milton Keynes UK
UKOW04f0152280415

250471UK00002B/48/P

9 781844 712816